Sports Publishing L.L.C.

Publisher: **Peter L. Bannon**
Senior Managing Editors: **Susan M. Moyer and Joseph J. Bannon Jr.**
Art Director: **K. Jeffrey Higgerson**
Senior Graphic Designer: **Kenneth J. O'Brien**
Developmental Editor: **Stephanie Fuqua**
Copy Editor: **Cynthia L. McNew**

Boston Herald

President and Publisher: **Patrick J. Purcell**
Editor: **Andrew F. Costello**
Executive Sports Editor: **Mark Torpey**
Director of Photography: **Garo Lachinian**
Vice President/Promotion: **Gwen Cage**
Chief Librarian: **John Cronin**

All stories and photographs are from the files of the *Boston Herald*.

Front cover photo: Kevork Djansezian
Back cover photo: Michael Seamans

ISBN: 1-58261-575-6

Printed in Mexico

Introduction

Nomar Garciaparra is a dangerous hitter who likes to take that first pitch and send it out to any area of the park that strikes his fancy. He is also a dominant and dynamic defensive presence on the field, with quick reactions and a strong arm.

He is—quite simply—an amazing, exciting baseball player.
Red Sox fans were energized about his playing before he ever got called up to the show. And once he joined the majors, he increased his fans' devotion by racking up award after award: Rookie of the Year, longest rookie hitting streak in the American League, All-Star shortstop and two-time AL batting champ.

Along with the highs have come the lows, most notably the 2001 season that saw Nomar on the DL and off the field for months after wrist surgery. But he's come back strong in 2002, and fans have been thrilled with the journey. They still chuckle over his superstitious rituals, flock to attend his autograph sessions, and debate every nuance of his game.

Nomar is a modest man, which is a refreshing trait in this age of conspicuous athletic hubris. And so he shakes off all career comparisons to Red Sox legend Ted Williams. But the comparisons will continue to be made long after Nomar has made his own marks in the annals of baseball history.

Stephanie Fuqua
Developmental Editor

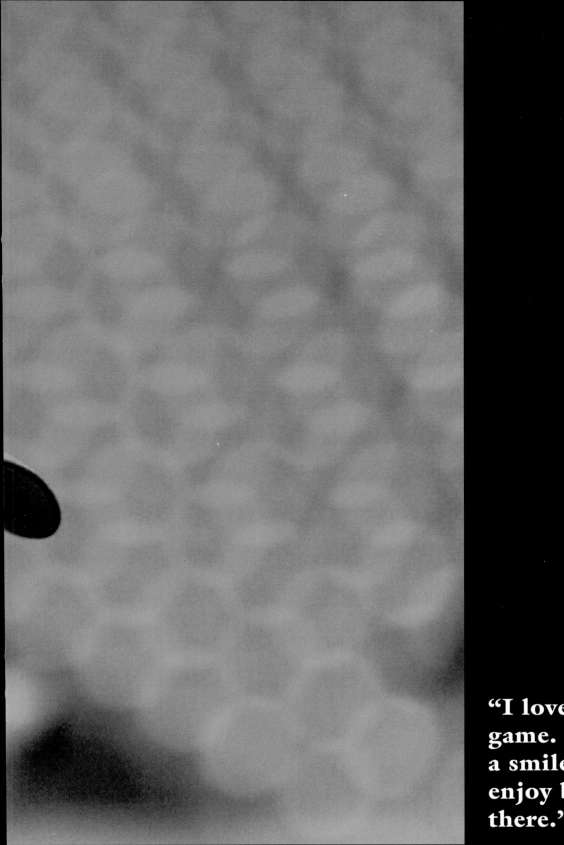

"I love playing the game. The game puts a smile on my face. I enjoy being out there."

Nomar Gets the Call

By Tony Massarotti

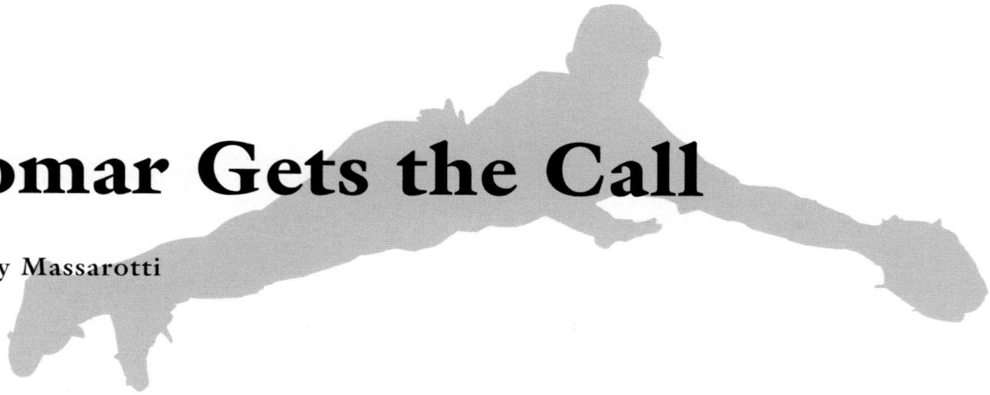

The wheels were turning in the Red Sox clubhouse last night. Two new faces had already arrived. Were more on the way?

Prior to the second game of a three-game series with the Oakland A's at the Coliseum, the Sox began shuffling their roster in anticipation of the midnight deadline for playoff eligibility. Manager Kevin Kennedy and assistant general manager Mike Port had planned meetings with several players as the Sox moved toward finalizing their roster.

Among the changes:

Shortstop Nomar Garciaparra has been called up from Pawtucket and added to the 25-man roster. Garciaparra immediately becomes eligible for the postseason. He replaces first baseman Greg Pirkl, who was designated for assignment.

Garciaparra said he is surprised to learn of his promotion following Pawtucket's game Friday night because he assumed he would remain with the PawSox for the International League playoffs.

"I thought I'd be staying around," he said. "It did take me by surprise—a nice surprise, though."

His promotion clearly struck a nerve with at least one Sox player—current shortstop John Valentin. Most believe Garciaparra will become the everyday shortstop next season, meaning Valentin would move to a new position. But Valentin still bristles at the idea of changing positions.

Said Valentin: "I'm not ready to move."

Valentin openly admits that he so strongly wants to play shortstop that he would consider playing elsewhere if the Sox cannot accommodate him.

"I want to stay with the Red Sox as a shortstop," he said. "But I'm not ruling out any options."

Garciaparra Steps Up

By Tony Massarotti

The bad news is the 1996 season appears to be over. The good news is that at least part of the future looks bright.

For the second time in two games, rookie phenom Nomar Garciaparra sparkled in the Red Sox' backbreaking 12-11 loss to the New York Yankees yesterday. Garciaparra went 2 for 5 with a triple and two RBIs. On Friday night, he went 2 for 3 with a pair of steals in the Sox' 4-2 win.

Sox manager Kevin Kennedy was disappointed by the meltdown of his young pitching staff in front of a stadium crowd of 54,559, but his young shortstop remained cool.

"I think he's doing a good job," Kennedy said of Garciaparra. "He's going to Puerto Rico [for winter ball] and that's going to help him. He's done a good job this month."

Kennedy made a point of referencing Garciaparra's plans to play this winter because a handful of younger Sox pitchers are reportedly reluctant to make that sacrifice. Kennedy refused to name winter-ball candidates, but left-hander Vaughn Eshelman and right-hander Joe Hudson are believed to be among them.

"When we ask people to go to winter ball, we do it because we think it will help them to help our ballclub," Kennedy said.

"He's the most superstitious guy I've ever seen," said Dennis Eckersley. "I mean, good Lord."

Nomar Goes with the Flow

By Tony Massarotti

Nomar Garciaparra barely caused a stir when he walked into the Red Sox' minor-league complex shortly before 3 p.m. yesterday, and he intends to keep it that way. He is far too smart to say something he could regret and far too secure to question his own abilities. He just wants to play and let everything else take care of itself.

"I'm coming in here with an open mind. I think that's the way everybody's coming in here," Garciaparra said while storing his belongings in his locker.

"All I can do is worry about myself so I'm ready for Opening Day. I can't say this should be going on or that should be going on. That's not for me to worry about. All I can worry about is getting into shape or putting on another five pounds, things like that."

John Valentin is the Sox' starting shortstop, arguably one of the best in the game at his position, and Garciaparra is the team's super-prospect at short. Unfortunately, there seems to be only one place for the two players, given Valentin's unwillingness to change positions and Garciaparra's reputation as a can't-miss kid.

Clearly, it is a bizarre circumstance. Two years ago, Valentin became just the fourth player in team history to have at least 20 homers and 20 steals in the same season, yet it is Garciaparra who will be featured in an upcoming issue of *Vanity Fair* that will focus on baseball's stars of tomorrow. Somewhere, something has to give.

Garciaparra said he hasn't "paid much attention" to the swirl surrounding the Sox' shortstop problem, but be sure that he knows the score. Garciaparra is ready for the big leagues and he knows it. He has been a shortstop "since freshman year in high school" and nobody has ever asked him to change positions.

"I guess this is the way baseball is and you have to deal with it," Garciaparra said. "Baseball is a game of adjustments on the field and it's a game of adjustments off the field, too. If I have to wait my turn, that's the way it is. I guess I just focus on the things I can control."

Would he be willing to play second base if the Sox elected to keep Valentin at short?

"We talked about that last year and I didn't see second," said Garciaparra. "I've never played second and I don't know what it feels like."

Garciaparra is treading lightly because baseball's behavioral code demands it. Rookies are not allowed to play their own trumpets when they reach the majors. If they do so, their teammates tune them out.

How diplomatic is Garciaparra trying to be? When asked if he would be disappointed to open the season in Triple A—where no one expects him to be—he chose the safest route.

"That's kind of tough," Garciaparra said. "We're all coming into a new situation. There's a whole new staff and there's new opinions. I'm not better than anyone else, I'm just different. I don't want to come in here and say I should be here or I should be there."

Garciaparra has put on five pounds, bringing his weight to an even 180. He has added roughly 20 pounds of muscle since the spring of 1995, greatly increasing his strength and stamina while leaving him as fat-free as a gymnast.

In spring training last year, Garciaparra tore apart opposing pitching before spraining his ankle on St. Patrick's Day. He opened the season at Pawtucket, then missed most of the summer when he suffered a tear to the hamstring tendon behind his left knee. Nonetheless, he finished the Triple A season with a .343 average, 16 homers and 46 RBIs in 172 at-bats before making his big-league debut as a late-season call-up. Now, he is ready, willing and able to play every day in the major leagues.

He just won't say so.

"Getting hurt last year was kind of a shock for me," Garciaparra said.

"This winter, I wanted to go out and rehab [the injury] so I don't even have to think about it when I'm out [on the field]. I did that."

He doesn't want to think about anything off the field, either. He would rather just play and take his chances.

Business as Usual

By Michael Silverman

Nomar Garciaparra got a major job promotion Saturday when the Red Sox named him their starting shortstop.

As he sees it, it's just business as usual.

"Nothing's going to change; I'm not going to change," said Garciaparra.

"I'm not going to go, 'Oh, I'm this now,' or, 'This is happening.' It's not going to change me. I'm just going to go out there and work hard."

Garciaparra is well aware of the career crisis Valentin is faced with and is taking no pleasure in it.

"I think it will be fine; he's a great individual, you all know that," said Garciaparra.

"I've always said I'm not better than him and he's not better than me. I don't really believe that I'm better than anybody; it's just a matter of opinion."

The opinion on Garciaparra is that he is already the smoothest and most natural-looking shortstop to play the position for the Sox in recent memory. He moves to the ball with gazelle-like quickness, and no matter into what position he has to contort his lean, 6-foot frame to scoop up a ball, the motion is fluid and effortless.

He simply is exciting to watch. He's a natural.

"I think things just fall in place for me," he said. "When I walk away every day from the game, I don't need numbers or any stats to tell me, 'Well, how did you do?' or 'What was your game like?' I don't buy into that. I can have a great game and go 0 for 4.

"I just wanted to know what's going on. Now I know I can go out and prepare myself differently, and go out there and prepare myself for Opening Day and be smart about it."

Nomar Touches All Bases

By George Kimball

Going up and down the dugout steps, he looks like a man attempting to pass a field sobriety test. Even though the wooden steps at City of Palms Park are no more than six inches high, Nomar Garciaparra minces his way up and down, bringing his feet together on each and every stair.

Watching Garciaparra take the field can also be a treat. Many baseball players, major-leaguers included, consider it bad luck to step on the baseline. Nomar takes this superstition to another level. He leaps over the entire basepath.

Nomar at the bat is another matter entirely. In a ritual that is likely to infuriate opposing pitchers and test the patience of at least a few American League umpires, Garciaparra employs a maddening preshot routine worthy of Jack Nicklaus.

Step back out of the batter's box. Kick dirt with each toe. With bat perched on left shoulder, adjust right batting glove. Adjust left batting glove. Touch uniform. Touch batting helmet. Get back in box.

And, mind you, this is whether he's swung at the pitch or not. A very fine line separates the creature of habit from the prisoner of superstition, and at 23, Garciaparra would appear perilously close to crossing it. Not at all, says Nomar.

The complicated entry/exit from the dugout, for instance, has a ready explanation: "I just don't want to trip going down the steps."

Presumably Nomar had a bad accident in the past, or witnessed one when somebody's spikes slipped out from under him? "No," said Garciaparra. "Just being careful, that's all."

And the running broad jump on his way out to shortstop?

"Lots of players try not to step on the line," said Garciaparra, who obviously isn't taking any chances.

Second nature though it may have become, Garciaparra admits he probably couldn't write down a list of the things he does in the batter's box without going through it first.

"I've been playing baseball since I was five, and soccer since I was six," he said. "There are just things you acquire over the years. You get into a routine and you don't want to mess with it. You want to feel exactly the same way every time.

"And me, I like to have everything nice and tight. I like my toes to reach the front of my shoes and my fingers to reach the end of the gloves. That's why I go through the things I do. I've had guys ask me what I'm doing, and I guess there are pitchers who think I'm taking too long, but really I don't.

"If you'll notice, I keep one foot in the batter's box all the time when I'm doing the other stuff. I've done that since college, when they called an automatic strike on me once."

The oddest part of it is that Garciaparra doesn't consider any of this behavior odd at all.

"I guess I don't even pay attention to it," he said. "It's part of my preparation and baseball is a game of routines. Everybody does things that make them comfortable and they develop into . . . habits.

Superstitions are nothing new to baseball, of course. God knows Wade Boggs harbored enough of them to keep an entire coven busy. But you'd think the everyday ballpark hex would be acquired through years of experience.

"Not necessarily," said Cardinals manager Tony La Russa. "I think all players, even young players, have their own little rituals. They may not be as noticeable or as extreme as his, but whether it's touching a certain base on your way to the field or dressing or undressing a certain way, most all of them do something."

"It can border on compulsive behavior," said Sox broadcaster Jerry Remy.

"When I played for the Red Sox," confessed Remy, "I had to take my whole uniform off one day after I realized I put my right sock on before the left one."

"You develop these routines because you want to feel the same way every time," Garciaparra attempted to explain. "When things are going good you want to do it exactly the same way you did it last time."

And when things aren't going good, you alter the routine?

"No. You get rid of everything else," he said with a laugh. "Take it all off. Get rid of these gloves. Get rid of this bat. But the routine stays the same."

Nomar is Starry-Eyed

By Michael Silverman

Four months ago, rookie Nomar Garciaparra remained calm as a spring training storm swirled around his arrival as the starting Red Sox shortstop.

Yesterday, after being named the Sox' sole representative for the All-Star Game on Tuesday in Cleveland, Garciaparra was equally unfazed.

Maybe it's a good thing Garciaparra has ice in his veins. Maybe that's what's helped him become the hottest rookie in the league.

"I think everyone likes to be respected," said Garciaparra, 23. "I appreciate the honor, but I don't see myself above anyone else. People have a decision to make and they make them."

The decision came from AL manager Joe Torre, who picked Garciaparra to become the first Sox rookie named to the squad since Fred Lynn in 1975, and their sixth rookie overall.

Once club leader Mo Vaughn became a nonfactor for selection after undergoing knee surgery, Garciaparra jumped to the front of the line.

He has consistently sparkled on defense with his range, glove work and throwing. While defense remains his most valuable asset, his offense has been more surprising.

The 12 homers and 42 RBIs he carried into last night's game against the Florida Marlins both ranked second on the club. He led the Sox in virtually all other offensive stats, including runs, hits, multihit games, triples, stolen bases and at-bats.

"He deserves to be on that team, he really does," said Sox manager Jimy Williams. "I really think that even if Mo was still here, he still deserves to go."

John Valentin also voiced his support for Garciaparra.

"I think it's wonderful, he's well-deserving," said Valentin. "He pretty much did it on his own. He's a new face in this league and he's surprised a lot of people."

Nomar Gets In on Fun

By Joe Giuliotti

It was a whirlwind 48 hours for Red Sox shortstop Nomar Garciaparra.

His first All-Star Game experience was one he will never forget: the congratulatory messages, the thrill of having his father share in his excitement the past two days, getting into the game and being on the winning side.

It was, as he said after the American League's 3-1 victory at Jacobs Field last night, "Great."

Garciaparra, the Sox' lone All-Star representative, sat for six innings. When he finally got the call from American League manager Joe Torre in the top of the seventh, he did everything he wanted to do.

He did his thing with the batting gloves, he tap danced in the batter's box, and yes, folks, he even swung at the first pitch from the New York Mets' Bobby Jones in the eighth.

"I thought about taking the first pitch, but why change?" Garciaparra said. "I probably would have shocked everybody if I took it."

The rookie's big smile after the game told the story.

"Great," he said when asked to sum up his two days mingling with the best of the best.

"I enjoyed it," said the 23-year-old, who won the inaugural rookie home run hitting contest on Monday. "I'm still enjoying it, enjoying everything about it, the excitement, everything."

His Sox teammates told him to have fun during the All-Star festivities, and he followed their advice to the letter.

"It was great," he said. "The crowd cheering like it did. It was a thrill, and the rush you got from the crowd was something."

Garciaparra watched from the AL dugout while Seattle's Alex Rodriguez manned the position for the first six innings. He said the wait actually calmed him down a bit.

"I was still a little nervous, but I was more nervous during the home run hitting contest," he said. "It was a different feeling."

Garciaparra, the first Sox rookie to be selected to an All-Star team since Fred Lynn in 1975, had one chance in the field—a popup by Chicago Cubs first baseman Mark Grace. In his one at-bat, he forced Brady Anderson at second on a grounder to third.

There was no hiding his youthful enthusiasm, from the home run hitting contest (he qualified for the main event by winning the rookie competition), to Monday night's All-Star Gala to the game itself. He said what made the two days even more special was the fact his father Ramon was able to spend it with him.

"I wish all my family could have been here, but it was much more special for me because my father was," he said.

Garciaparra also made sure not to repeat the mistake made by Mo Vaughn last year, when the Sox first baseman came home empty-handed from the All-Star Game in Philadelphia. Vaughn's teammates were all over him for his forgetfulness. Garciaparra did not forget to get the gifts.

"I ordered the T-shirts, and I want you to know they are being shipped to Fenway Park," said Garciaparra. "I have more than enough. I couldn't carry them, but they are being shipped."

Garciaparra didn't have any bonus clause in his contract for making the team, and that didn't faze him one bit.

"Who cares about the money?" he said. "I'd rather have this [experience] than the money. I play this game because I love it: being in that dugout, seeing everybody smiling and watching Sandy [Alomar] hit that [game-winning] home run. It was great for Sandy."

Garciaparra said it will probably be a few more days before everything really sinks in, and then it will seem like his All-Star debut went by all too fast. He said he has been deluged with calls congratulating him on being selected.

"I called my apartment back in Boston and my answering machine was filled with messages," he said. "There were a lot of calls. So many. I laughed and enjoyed them. I'm going to take the tape out of the machine and save it."

The normally quiet Garciaparra was talking a blue streak after the game. He was really caught up in the excitement of everything that happened. He certainly followed his teammates' advice—he had fun.

It's Unanimous: Nomar Voted Rookie of the Year

By Tony Massarotti

Some time in August, long after the Red Sox were eliminated from playoff contention, Nomar Garciaparra secured the American League Rookie of the Year award.

All that was left to be determined was whether anyone else would garner serious consideration.

The answer: Nomar in a landslide.

Capping off an extraordinary debut season in which he broke an assortment of team, league and baseball records, Garciaparra was unanimously named the AL Rookie of the Year. He joins outfielder Fred Lynn (1975), catcher Carlton Fisk (1972), pitcher Don Schwall (1961) and first baseman Walt Dropo (1950) as the only Sox players to win the award, though Fisk was the only other to sweep the polls. Aside from Garciaparra and Fisk, only four players have been unanimous Rookie of the Year selections in the 49 years the AL has distributed the award.

"You only get a chance at it one time. You're only a rookie once," Garciaparra said. "To get this honor, it means an awful lot."

Said Sox general manager Dan Duquette: "The Red Sox are real proud of the year that Nomar Garciaparra had for us. It was a terrific year, a storybook year, really. He's just a great asset to the team and he's got a great future ahead of him with the Red Sox."

Added Sox manager Jimy Williams: "Well-deserved, well-earned. Great work ethic on a daily basis, offensively and defensively. He prepares himself to help the team win a game."

With all he has already done, Garciaparra somehow plans to get better.

"I'm not really satisfied. I think there's room for improvement everywhere, offensively and defensively," he said.

"I love playing. Nothing gives me greater joy than being on the field and playing against the best. Every kid grows up wanting to play against the best."

"I take pride day in and day out when I put on that uniform. I represent not only myself, but my teammates and the whole city. And I want to go out there and do the best I can for them."

Nomar Agrees to $23M Deal

By Michael Silverman and Tony Massarotti

Nomar Garciaparra's unprecedented rookie year paid off with an unprecedented contract yesterday, as the shortstop and Red Sox agreed to terms on a five-year deal worth a guaranteed $23.25 million. The club holds options for 2003 and 2004 that would bring the total value to $45.25 million.

"He has all the attributes our fans adore," said Sox general manager Dan Duquette. "This is a complete player. From the bottom of his soles to the top of his head, he's a baseball player. His whole life is dedicated to baseball—from the time he gets up in the morning, when he gets to sleep, what he eats—everything he does is dedicated to being a baseball player.

"He's got a great work ethic, good leadership ability. He has long-term goals. He's everything you want a ballplayer to be."

Garciaparra sat to Duquette's left during the press conference announcing the agreement, and the two were flanked by hitting coach Jim Rice and new guest instructor Luis Aparicio. After listening to Duquette's praise, which included comparisons to Rice's power ability and Aparicio's glovework, Garciaparra said, "I just want to meet this guy you're talking about—wow. This is quite an honor. I'm very flattered.

"This means a lot to me," Garciaparra added. "The Red Sox have shown a commitment to me and I want to show my commitment to them for a while. I really like the city and the whole surroundings. It's an honor, and, like they said, I don't have to worry about anything now and can just play baseball for the next five years."

Garciaparra's pact shatters the previous high for a player with one year of experience—National League Rookie of the Year Scott Rolen signed a four-year, $10 million deal with Philadelphia earlier this spring.

Duquette said Garciaparra's gifts were so promising the club wanted to get a deal done sooner rather than later, based in good part on the ever-spiraling salaries across the major leagues.

"We're paying him at today's market rate," said Duquette. "We feel Nomar will improve."

Negotiations, which had been rumored to be near completion for weeks, picked up steam last month.

"If there was any pivotal meeting [with the Red Sox], it was at the NBA All-Star Game in New York [last month]," said Garciaparra's agent, Arn Tellem. "That's when we got into specifics and started moving it along."

The deal is still not signed and sealed, but Garciaparra will make $600,000 this season (he made $150,000 last year), $900,000 in 1999, $3.3 million in 2000, $6.85 million in 2001 and $8.6 million in 2002. The 24-year-old Georgia Tech product will receive a $2 million signing bonus. There is also a buyout clause after the fifth year worth $1 million.

The deal includes club options for 2003 worth $10.5 million and 2004 for $11.5 million. In each option year, however, the base would increase by $500,000 if Garciaparra gains a berth in the All-Star Game four times in the next five seasons. The Sox must decide whether to exercise the first option by Opening Day of the 2000 season.

The swiftness with which the deal was struck stands in stark contrast to the muddle the club is in with Mo Vaughn, who wants his own long-term deal. While those talks have become acrimonious, there was only good feeling in the air yesterday.

"It's nice to get some security and at the same time, throughout these negotiations, it wasn't a bad one," said Garciaparra. "Both parties felt happy."

Garciaparra said he is still studying which charities he plans to work with in the years to come. Duquette mentioned that Garciaparra's father Ramon, a graphic artist, will design a commemorative Garciaparra bat.

Shortstop Shines as Sophomore

By Tony Massarotti

The show is now in its second full season, still playing to a chorus of rave reviews. The legend only seems to grow with Nomar Garciaparra. The luster doesn't seem to fade.

Eight months after a unanimous selection as American League Rookie of the Year, Garciaparra is once again sizzling as the Red Sox prepare to open a three-game series with the Montreal Expos tonight. His latest hitting streak stands at 20 games, tying the longest run in the majors this season. With each passing day, the streak gets longer and the praise gets louder.

Many have already seen Garciaparra perform, of course. Others are seeing his act for the first time.

"He's a great player, man, but that's not what really impresses me about Nomar. You can tell that he has a lot of ability," said first-year Sox outfielder Darren Lewis, an eight-year major-league veteran who played with the Chicago White Sox and Los Angeles Dodgers last season.

"He's always the same [mentally], and for a young player, he really knows how to play the game. A lot of players come up and they have the talent, but their baseball intellect isn't very good. That's just a credit to his intelligence.

"Obviously, he works very hard," said Lewis. "Playing with him every day, you can see that he's a fierce competitor. I don't think there's anything that's going to get in his way and slow him down. He's that competitive. He wants to do well and he wants to win. There's nothing that's going to stop him. You can just see it in his eyes every day."

Said Sox reliever Dennis Eckersley, who played in St. Louis last year and is now in his 24th major-league season: "I had heard a lot about him—incredible [stuff]—but you don't believe it until you see it."

And now?

"I'm impressed," answered the Eck.

Immune to the Jinx

The second year is supposed to be more difficult. Flaws are detected and weaknesses are exposed. Expectations increase and performance declines. That said, Garciaparra appears to be getting better this year. Entering tonight's game against Montreal, he is batting .316 with 11 home runs and 49 RBIs. With nearly a week remaining until the midseason break, he has essentially duplicated his first-half performance from last season, when totals of .291, 13 and 44 landed him in the All-Star Game.

Remember, too, that Garciaparra has missed 16 games with a shoulder separation that forced him to the disabled list for the first time in his career.

As Lewis said, nothing seems to stop him.

"I couldn't tell you right now if I was better or worse than last year," Garciaparra said. "I missed quite a bit because I was injured, but you have to deal with it. I feel better because our team is playing better and because of where we're at team-wise. I'm being utilized a little different by batting third and there are certain things to adjust to. That could be a factor in certain things, too.

"I think I just took what I did last year and prepared myself again this year. I think what I learned is how many adjustments you have to make. Some work and some don't."

Thus far, most of Garciaparra's adjustments are working. Sox manager Jimy Williams has batted Garciaparra first, second, third and fourth this season, and at no time has Garciaparra seemed out of place. Over the weekend, while the Sox were in Miami, Williams acknowledged that such versatility is what makes Garciaparra truly special.

Garciaparra's only real statistical drop-off has come on the basepaths this season. After recording 13 steals before the All-Star break last season, he has just six this year. He has attempted just 10 steals, though that number has more to do with the fact that he is batting third—directly ahead of Mo Vaughn—than with a decrease in efficiency.

Beyond that, he has been his usual self, offensively and defensively.

Maybe better.

"After he was raking in the first half [last year], I said, 'We'll see how he is the second time around—that will show how good he is,' " said Sox reliever Jim Corsi. "But guess what? It didn't matter then and it doesn't matter this year. He's got a quick bat and he hits the ball to all fields. He's making the adjustments.

"I think he's gotten a little better defensively, too, believe it or not. He probably has more errors [11], but he's made a lot of great plays."

A Hitting Machine

In his career Garciaparra already has had seven hitting streaks of 10 games or more. The current 20-gamer is the second-longest of his career, trailing only the AL rookie record 30-game streak he set during the second half of last season.

Consistency? Garciaparra has had at least one hit in 54 of the 62 games he's played this season, and only once has he gone hitless in consecutive games (June 5-6).

Garciaparra has played in 215 games since the start of last year and hit safely in 172, a staggering efficiency rate of 80 percent.

Roughly six days a week, the sun rises, the sun sets, Lou Gorman has lunch and Garciaparra gets a hit.

On the seventh day, Nomar rests.

"He can hit a lot of different pitches," Williams said. "He can hit a lot of pitches that maybe aren't in the strike zone, but they're pitches that he can hit hard. I'm not sure how you pitch the kid."

Said Garciaparra: "You want to be able to contribute all the way through [the season]. That's important to me."

Mum's the Word

As always, Garciaparra has refused to discuss the streak. He refuses, in fact, to even say the word. After each game recently, he has stood before his locker and requested that he be asked no questions about "statistics."

It is just one his many quirks, a list that often includes eating the same sandwich—ham and cheese—before games.

"He's the most superstitious guy I've ever seen," said Eckersley. "I mean, good Lord."

Garciaparra's teammates, for their part, similarly do everything in their power to avoid jinxing their teammate. Garciaparra has defended his rituals by saying baseball is a game of "routines."

Many of his teammates subscribe to similar methods, though none is quite as obvious. Still, be sure that they are watching closely. Corsi recently admitted as much.

"I'm rooting for the kid. How can you not root for him?" Corsi said. "He's very humble and he's got a great sense of humor. He's not cocky. You want him to shine."

He paused.

"He's like a regular schmo," Corsi said.

That might be a stretch.

Leading the Masses

By Michael Silverman

In his short two-year career, Nomar Garciaparra has consistently dazzled with his tremendous offensive and defensive skills.

Last night, he showcased a new facet—leadership.

While the Red Sox season ended in the 2-1 Game 4 Division Series loss to the Indians, Garciaparra was the picture of genuine emotion and class behavior.

As the Sox were going down in order in the bottom of the ninth, Garciaparra was on top of the dugout steps, back to the field, beseeching the crowd to get into the game by clapping his hands hard.

After the Indians won, Garciaparra was on the field, waiting to hug each and every member of the bullpen trudging off. Then, he turned and gave a round of applause to the Fenway faithful.

"I wanted to thank them for believing in us all year," said Garciaparra. "This is what it's all about. I appreciated them and I think they appreciated what we did on the field. I was telling them thank you, I was telling them thank you for being here all year for us. We have to thank them."

Garciaparra's teammate, Dennis Eckersley, has quietly watched Garciaparra's MVP-quality efforts this season. What he saw postgame left the Eck thinking there is still room to blossom for the 25-year-old, who may find himself the player-leader next season.

"Maybe it's happening," said Eckersley. "Some people are not meant to be that, but with him, I don't know. He's very professional for his age. At his age, I was . . . I was, let's say, different. I like what I see."

Garciaparra obviously derived motivation from his belief that the media were doubters about this year's team. He drew strength from it again last night.

"We're not disappointed. We're not going to hang our heads," he said. "You guys said we were not going to do anything this year and look at what we did."

A Reluctant Leader

By Steve Buckley

Chained at the ankles and nudged along by armed representatives of the Lee County Sheriff's Dept., Nomar Garciaparra yesterday held his first press conference of spring training.

Mo Vaughn or no Mo Vaughn, Garciaparra hates these things. He'd rather have a tooth pulled, or, worse, be forced to parade around camp in the black double-breasted suit Red Sox general manager Dan Duquette was wearing yesterday than to have to make light conversation with the writers and TV people.

But let the record show that Garciaparra was polite, cordial, and at times even humorous yesterday.

There was no joking, however, when he adamantly refused he is the one who will take up the leadership torch left behind by Anaheim's newest Angel, Mo Vaughn.

Garciaparra slam-dunked the ongoing assumption that he must somehow step up and replace the departed Vaughn, both on the field and in front of the cameras. When it was put to Garciaparra that with Mo gone he is now "The Man," the Red Sox shortstop made it clear he is no such thing.

"I don't know what 'The Man's' definition is," he said. "People say 'The Man' or whatever. Nobody's 'The Man.' Baseball's the game, and that's all there is to it. We go out there and play the game. There's no such thing as 'The Man.' Nobody's bigger than the game.

"It's just a game, and I go out and play hard and to the best of my ability. And that's all I can do. I play for the Boston Red Sox. I take pride day in and day out when I put on that uniform. I represent not only myself, but my teammates and the whole city. And I want to go out there and do the best I can for them."

In the matter of Mo, Garciaparra minces no words: "You can't replace a guy like Mo, no matter what. But nobody's looking to do that. Nobody's going to say, 'All right, I'm Mo Vaughn,' or I'm this or I'm that.

"Everybody's still themselves, and we still have a great ballclub. Everybody has the same personality. Nobody's going to change. They don't need to change. We'll come out here and prepare ourselves for the season like any other year."

Garciaparra is filled with optimism. The writers may see dark skies, but Nomar sees sunshine. He likes the pitching, he likes the defense, and, yes, he likes the offense. Whatever anyone else may think of the Sox, he sees a solid team.

"The good thing is that I don't read headlines or read reports," he said. "But they did that last year, so what's the difference? It's the same thing as last year. Everybody was writing us off. The only guys who supported us last year were our teammates and our fans, and look what we gave them. And we were disappointed. We feel we should have done more. Our goal is to win the World Series."

This I-don't-read-the-reports business is an ever-popular throwaway line from Garciaparra. He's always quick to point out that he doesn't follow what people write about the Red Sox, remarking yesterday, "I don't pay attention to it. Why should I waste my energy on that when I know what's going on myself? I'm in there. I know exactly what's going on all around the team, so I don't need somebody else to tell me something, because they don't know, being on the outside looking in."

We could argue with Garciaparra on this point. On the one hand, he's always whining about negative coverage and how nobody picked the Red Sox to win last year; on the other hand, he's always saying he doesn't read "the reports."

But, hey, it's spring training, everybody loves Nomar, and why quibble?

As for his comments yesterday, they were lovely and delivered with emotion. Surely what he said is how he feels. A man's words are his words.

What will not change, though, is that Garciaparra from this day forward is the heart and soul of the Red Sox. Just as this team was once defined by Mo Vaughn, and before that Roger Clemens, and before that Jim Rice, and before that Carl Yastrzemski, and before that Ted Williams, the Red Sox now are defined by Nomar Garciaparra.

Frankly, he has no say in the matter. This is the Nomar Garciaparra Era in the annals of Red Sox history.

Sorry, Nomar, but you are . . . "The Man."

Nomar Reaches New Heights

By Tony Massarotti

We always knew the kid might make some history, maybe break a few records. We just had no idea that Nomar Garciaparra would try to do it all in one day.

In another eye-popping installment to what is fast becoming an extraordinary career, Garciaparra launched a one-man assault on the Red Sox record book at wild and windy Fenway Park last night. He hit three home runs. He had two grand slams. He finished the night with 10 RBIs as the Sox whipped the Seattle Mariners 12-4.

Mercy.

The legend grows.

"It was amazing," a giddy Garciaparra said after the game. "I've never in my life hit three home runs, let alone two grand slams. It was something else. I was crossing the plate [after the second grand slam] and I was looking at the guys. I didn't know what to say. I was speechless.

"Days like this, you enjoy them," Garciaparra said. "I don't take anything for granted."

See? We always knew the kid was smart, too. Garciaparra has rarely acknowledged his personal achievements since reaching the big leagues in 1996, but even he could not contain himself last night. Nomar could finish this career in the Hall of Fame, go to heaven and be reincarnated as himself, but he is wise enough to realize the rarity of this latest feat.

Two grand slams in a game? Only two other Sox players have done it—Jim Tabor (1939) and Rudy York (1946)—and neither was a shortstop. Three other Sox players have collected 10 RBIs—York, Norm Zauchin (1955) and Fred Lynn (1975)—but none of them played in the middle of the infield, either.

"Special game, to say the least. Two grand slams. Ten RBIs. It's special to have the opportunity to watch something like that," said Sox manager and baseball lifer Jimy Williams. "I can't recall [seeing] a game where somebody drove in 10 runs. I've seen three home runs before, but not 10 RBIs."

Naturally, the performance was not lost on an announced Fenway crowd of 21,660, which demanded a curtain call from Garciaparra after his second grand slam in the eighth. Garciaparra obliged them by trotting up the steps of the dugout and waving his helmet—"I think the fans here are awesome," he said—a distinctive Fenway moment if ever there was one.

So what are we to make of this team now? The Red Sox have been dull and dispiriting for much of this season, but there is no denying the fever that has enveloped Fenway over the last several days. First Mo Vaughn returned. Then Pedro Martinez struck out 15. Then Juan Pena sparkled in his major-league debut.

Now comes Nomar, who has only grown in size and stature since the Red Sox plucked him out of Georgia Tech with their first-round pick (12th overall) in the 1994 draft.

"He was a little bigger and a little stronger, but he hit home runs then, too. He hit balls out to right center," said catcher Jason Varitek, who played alongside Garciaparra for three years in college. "He was a great hitter from the day he set foot on the campus. You add a little age and maturity, and now you've got what you've got."

And what you've got is a whirlwind. Garciaparra has played in Boston for a little more than two full seasons, winning a unanimous Rookie of the Year award in 1997 and a silver medal in the MVP balloting last summer. He is still only 25, for goodness sake, and he is already evoking comparisons with the greatest players in club history.

Know what the truly amazing part is? Entering last night's game, Garciaparra was batting .309 with two home runs and 14 RBIs, and, as Varitek pointed out, "everyone knows he's not even close to being locked in yet." Shortly after getting dressed, Garciaparra was sitting in front of his locker saying that wasn't entirely comfortable at the plate, that he still had to work to do.

Then came the grand slam into the Seattle bullpen in the first. Then came the two-run homer around the right-field foul pole in the third. Then he came to the plate in the eighth, with the bases loaded again, with the fans bubbling with anticipation.

First pitch, screen job.

"I probably would have swung at anything," Garciaparra said. "If they had thrown it 10 feet over my head, I probably would have swung. There was a lot of energy going on there."

Of course, he was the one causing it.

ALL★STAR
AMERICAN
P
1 2 3 4 5 6 7 8 9 10
R H
40 TB
61 BOSTON
AT BAT BALL STRIKE OUT
53 MIN
46 CLE

Fenway's Greatest Work of Art?

By Michael Gee

Not for the first time, Nomar Garciaparra confronted the bane of his existence. He was in the presence of another human being who failed to comprehend baseball.

The Red Sox shortstop was asked yesterday if there were any tricks to being a successful Home Run Derby participant. At the word "trick," Garciaparra smiled, not with pleasure, and rolled his eyes to the ceiling.

"No trick," Garciaparra said emphatically. "When you play this game there are no tricks."

How odd that a magical talent doesn't believe in tricks. But to Garciaparra, the notion that his game holds secrets is heresy. Baseball is all so obvious to him. Why can't others see it as he does, feel and appreciate the game as he does?

Garciaparra's wish is the genius and curse of every creative artist. They see and feel things the rest of us cannot. That's what enables their art to change the way others see and feel. But that's also why great artists have been known to go nuts.

That Garciaparra is an artist is beyond doubt. In two and a half seasons in the major leagues, he has established himself as one of the rare athletes who can make his sport a creative medium, a means of self-expression. Garciaparra's play says who he is.

And that play says Garciaparra is in the early days of a career that would seem to have no known limits. After winning the 1997 Rookie of the Year award with one of the finest offensive seasons any shortstop ever had, Garciaparra was even better in '98.

This season, batting in a lineup that struggles to score, Garciaparra's been better yet. His .366 average, 14 homers, and 57 RBIs are the linchpin of the Sox' attack, as we have seen during his recent nine-game absence with a strained left groin.

When Garciaparra was apprenticing in the minors after being Dan Duquette's first first-round draft pick in 1994, the buzz went that he was such a fine fielder, he'd be

an All-Star if he hit .260. Now, of course, if Garciaparra hit .260 for just two weeks it'd be a catastrophe for the Red Sox.

Not that the buzz was wrong about Garciaparra's glove. After a rash of throwing errors in '98, Garciaparra's fielding has returned to its essentially flawless norm, a beautiful combination of range, athleticism, and a 105mm howitzer attached to his right shoulder. He is a contender for a truly rare combination, a Gold Glove shortstop who leads the league in slugging percentage.

Here's another heresy that will cause Garciaparra more frustration with an ignorant world. Shortstops are more important than left fielders. Given

health, Nomar has a chance to become the premier Red Sox player of all time, ahead of Ted Williams. He's shown himself capable of that much.

Garciaparra's not a tortured artist, mind you. He wasn't going to cut off an ear to celebrate being voted the American League's starting shortstop for tonight's All-Star Game. For Nomar, baseball is so fulfilling, even its pains are part of the fun, or rather, they are part of the experience that must be savored if the game is to be understood.

"Nobody knows the physical and mental anguish this game puts on you," Garciaparra said in the midst of a lengthy tribute to Cal Ripken. "You can't know unless you play. I didn't know until my first season in professional baseball."

Garciaparra was using "know" as an artist does, where feeling the answer means more than merely having it right. National icon Ripken hardly lacks for appreciation. Without the experience of walking a season in Ripken's cleats, however, Garciaparra doesn't think that appreciation is complete.

"I'm a fan as much as anybody," Garciaparra said. "I have a lot of respect for this game."

Respect is a big deal for Garciaparra, a touchstone of his outlook. He's an artist with a well-ordered, Apollonian idea of just how baseball should be played, watched, and perceived, combined with a sunny view of the sport that's equal parts John R. Tunis and Norman Rockwell.

In Garciaparra's view, players should do their best, enjoy themselves, and revel in the chance to participate in the creative process. Stars ("I'm not a celebrity") should act like everybody else, because, except for baseball, they are.

Fans should sit back and take in the fun. Garciaparra sees the customers as integral parts of his own experience.

"Fenway isn't Fenway Park until it's packed," Garciaparra said. "It's too bad some of the fans who support us day in and day out won't be at the All-Star Game."

Asked endlessly to compare himself to his fellow astonishing shortstops Derek Jeter and Alex Rodriguez, Garciaparra had three stock responses. He feels comparisons are odious. He is honored to be mentioned along with his peers. But then came the most revealing comment.

"It's a great time to be a fan," Garciaparra said more than once.

There's an artist's line for you. There's a lot of interesting work being done. Movies are better than ever. Or, in Nomar's mind, baseball is better than ever.

Is the jackrabbit ball responsible for the offensive explosion of the '90s? Not according to Garciaparra.

"Players are stronger," Garciaparra said. "They're faster. They do more things to get that edge. Not just hitters, pitchers. They're throwing the ball harder. So it goes faster when you hit it. That's just physics."

Garciaparra's bullish view of his business could be right. It's hard to look at the two rosters for tonight's game and not agree with him. From the standpoint of his own position, the evidence is clear. In the first 95 years of this century, there were exactly four shortstops who were dominant hitters—Honus Wagner, Ernie Banks, Joe Cronin and Cal Ripken. Now there are three at once.

Garciaparra is putting so much into baseball because he's capable of taking so much out of it. In word and deed, it's apparent that it fills him with a profound joy, an emotion that he's translated into a daily offering to others.

What is that but art? It's imprudent, but there was never a doubt Garciaparra would miss the All-Star Game. Without his work, the artist cannot exist.

"[The All-Star] experience will be more exciting when I get on the field," Garciaparra said. "When I'm in my element."

Renoir in the studio. Mozart at the harpsichord. Garciaparra at short.

No Mistaking Sox Pain

By Steve Conroy

The pain was obvious on Nomar Garciaparra's face.

Standing at his Fenway Park locker last night after the Red Sox' 6-1 Game 5 loss to the Yankees—which sent the dreaded New Yorkers to the World Series yet again—the Red Sox' shortstop addressed reporters in full uniform, apparently not wanting his spectacular season to end.

But end it did, and perhaps the hardest part was that the Sox themselves had as much to do with losing this series as the vaunted world champions. They committed a League Championship Series record 10 errors.

"We didn't lose to a better team," said Garciaparra. "We just didn't play well enough to win."

The tightness of the losses contributed to Garciaparra's pain.

"It had nothing to do with them being better. You can tell that with all the [close] games," he said. "That's what makes it tough, too, to see the games that we had in this series and they could have gone either way. We could have come back here, and it could have easily have been 3-0, us. Knowing how tight all the games were makes it harder to swallow a little bit. Sometimes you wish you just got blown out . . . But we didn't—and we didn't do that all year.

"You see it in these guys' eyes. You walk around the clubhouse and you see it. I've said it all year. We went out there and we played with a lot of heart. You can see it in every single guy's face."

While the shortstop is proud of his team and how it scrapped all year when people counted the Sox out at several junctures, it won't make it any easier to watch the World Series as a spectator again.

"I'm definitely just upset. I'm sad that it's all over," he said.

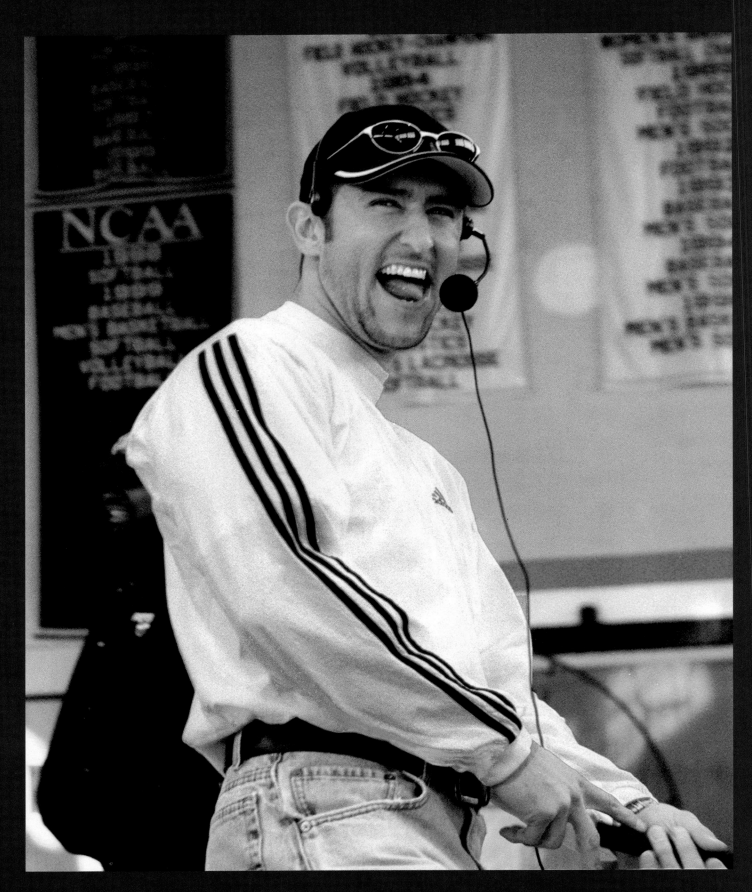

Nomar Springs Into Action

By Tony Massarotti

Nomar Garciaparra has been in the major leagues for only three full years, but his resume is already long and distinguished. He was the American League Rookie of the Year in 1997. He finished second in the Most Valuable Player award voting in 1998. Last year, he won his first batting title.

Still, he remains unfulfilled entering the spring of 2000.

"My goal is the same every year—I try to win a World Series," Garciaparra said yesterday at the Red Sox' minor-league facility, where he will join his teammates on the field this afternoon for the club's first full workout of spring training. "It's simple. That's my frame of mind. I try to win a World Series year in and year out."

The Red Sox just might have that chance this year, but don't expect Garciaparra to buy into the hype. Despite the addition of center fielder Carl Everett, Garciaparra does not believe the Sox look any more impressive on paper than they did a year ago at this time. But then, he had much higher hopes for the Sox than most as the team entered the spring of 1999.

So this year, like last, Garciaparra arrived in camp early, checking into the Sox' facility on Monday afternoon. He underwent his physical exam yesterday morning and reported that his body fat was measured at roughly five percent, placing him somewhere between Calista Flockhart and Cameron Diaz in the line at the salad bar.

As for the Red Sox, Garciaparra's confidence in the team hasn't waned one bit.

"I don't think we look better [than last year]. I think we look the same on paper," Garciaparra said. "I think it's different in the way people see us."

But perceptions change, naturally, which is something that Garciaparra has similarly come to learn. Roughly two years ago at this time, after his extraordinary rookie season, Garciaparra signed a five-year contract with the Sox worth a guaranteed $23.25 million. The deal contains a pair of club options—the Sox are obligated to exercise the first before April 1—that can bring the total value of the package to $45.25 over seven seasons, an average salary of just under $6.5 million per year.

Though Garciaparra's contract was a revolutionary deal for a player coming off his rookie season, the deal only seemed to shrink in magnitude this winter. New York Yankees shortstop Derek Jeter, after all, has been negotiating a seven-year deal that is said to be worth $118.5 million—an average of slightly more than $16.9 million per year—and as every Bostonian knows, Jeter is not $10 million per year better than Garciaparra.

Does Garciaparra regret agreeing to his contract?

"Absolutely not," he answered. "If [Jeter] gets what he gets, I'm happy for him. I'm happy with what I did [contractually] and I'm content with what I get. It was great to do at the time. If I look back, I would have done it the same way."

Would he expect the Sox to renegotiate his contract at some point?

"If they want to do it, it's up to them," Garciaparra said. "I don't worry about it."

For now, Garciaparra doesn't seem to be worrying about anything else, either. He has recovered from the right wrist injury that plagued him in the final weeks of the regular season and playoffs. He hopes to play this year without any of the nagging problems that have hindered him over the past two seasons. He believes the Red Sox can compete with the mighty New York Yankees.

He is staying focused on a familiar task.

"We didn't lose to a better team. We just didn't play good enough to win," he said of last season's loss to the Yankees in the American League Championship Series. "We understand what we have [as a team] and we understand each other's capabilities. We just go with that. That's all we can do."

Nomar Debut Short, Sweet

By Jeff Horrigan

With a player as extraordinary as Nomar Garciaparra, it was almost fitting that the ordinary was the only thing that gave him trouble in his spring training debut yesterday at City of Palms Park.

Garciaparra, who sprained his right knee during workouts on Feb. 25, led off and played three innings in the 9-8, 12-inning loss to the Philadelphia Phillies. He batted twice in the seven-run first inning and wasted no time picking up where he left off last October.

Garciaparra opened the bottom half of the first with a single up the middle off former All-Star Paul Byrd and scored the game's first run on Troy O'Leary's grand slam. He popped out in his second at-bat of the inning.

Garciaparra's only difficulties were with routine ground balls. Kevin Jordan bounced a two-out grounder to his right with two outs in the top of the first, allowing him to test the knee with a similar play to the one on which he suffered the injury. He scooted over and effortlessly fielded the ball but then short-hopped his throw across the diamond, where handcuffed first baseman Gary Gaetti was unable to come up with it.

Garciaparra was charged with an error on the play. He didn't have anything hit his way again until the third inning, when Jordan hit a nearly identical grounder to his right. Once again, Garciaparra bounced his throw to Gaetti, but this time the first baseman was able to control the throw. He said that he wasn't thinking about the knee on the plays and made no excuses for the poor throws.

"Maybe I was a little antsy . . . but I wasn't worried about anything and it's good that I can go out and not worry," Garciaparra said. "It was a good sign actually that I wasn't thinking about it."

Gaetti joked that he might want to think about improving his throws.

"Throw the ball," he grumbled with a laugh as he walked by Garciaparra, surrounded by reporters.

"I'm just testing you out to see what I've got over there," the shortstop shot back.

Garciaparra actually followed the second bouncer with one of his vintage defensive gems, which seemed to remove the final doubt about the knee. Rico Brogna lined a hard grounder into the hole and Garciaparra raced to his right, cleanly backhanded it and launched a laser on the run over to first.

"That's the easier ball, if you ask me," he said.

Garciaparra's sunny disposition throughout the 15-day layoff gave those who know him indication that the injury wasn't serious. Forever cautious manager Jimy Williams, however, insisted that he not try to rush back.

"I probably could have been back last week, but when they said, 'How does it feel?' and I said, 'It feels pretty good', they said, 'Good, take another week'," Garciaparra said. "If we were starting tomorrow, I'd have been in the games last week, but why rush when you don't have to?"

Because of the three-hour, cross-state bus journey required to get to today's game against the Montreal Expos in Jupiter, Garciaparra won't make his next appearance until tomorrow, when the Red Sox host the Toronto Blue Jays at City of Palms.

"I found out that I can do everything I need to do, so it's good to get the kinks out of the way," he said.

Garciaparra's return instantly resurrected the debate about where he should hit in the order. He batted third 33 times and cleanup in 100 games last year. Carl Everett, who is likely to hit third this season, said that Garciaparra would prefer batting fourth, but the defending American League batting champion said he has no real preference as long as he remains in one spot or the other.

"There's a rhythm to this game," he reasoned. "It's why everyone wants to stay in a consistent spot in the lineup. I'm used to [cleanup], but hit me third and I'll get used to that, too."

Nomar Put on 15-Day DL

By Jeff Horrigan

Nomar Garciaparra will be sidelined until at least May 27 after being placed on the 15-day disabled list for only the second time in his career. The move was made before the Red Sox' 9-0 shutout of the Orioles last night at Camden Yards.

The Red Sox shortstop, who aggravated a nagging left hamstring strain on Thursday, was replaced on the active roster by Pawtucket infielder Donnie Sadler. Garciaparra will be eligible to return for the middle of three games against the Yankees in New York later this month. He will continue to travel with the team in order to undergo treatment from the training staff.

"After 24 hours, you usually get a vibe as to how you're going to feel, and I'm pretty sore," he said. "I knew yesterday that I did it pretty bad. I definitely pulled something."

Garciaparra has been bothered by injuries in his four-year career, but he's had only one previous stint on the DL. That was in 1998 (May 9-27), when he was benched by a sprained right shoulder.

"It's very frustrating," he said. "I can't stand sitting down and having to watch a game when I can't play. It drives me crazy."

Nomar's Injury a Worry for Sox

By Mark Murphy

The collective worry that shot through Fenway last night at the sight of Nomar Garciaparra curled up in pain in shallow left field had nothing on the heavy tape job that covered the shortstop after last night's 4-2 win over the Yankees.

Starting with the huge package of ice strapped to Garciaparra's right shoulder, the wrapping spiraled around him like a tunic, reaching down to the ice packs in place on his left calf and his right ankle. Garciaparra injured the latter two areas in the seventh inning after tripping backward over center fielder Carl Everett while pulling in a Ricky Ledee pop-up.

The shortstop hit the ground hard, momentarily sat back up to throw the ball in to second baseman Jeff Frye, and then rolled back over in obvious pain. He not only turned his right ankle while making the catch but also took a shot to the back of his calf, courtesy of Everett's knee.

"I'm not sure I'm going to get a good night's sleep tonight," Garciaparra said.

The Red Sox begin a three-game series in Toronto tonight, though it's anyone's guess as to Garciaparra's status for the game.

"It's all right right now, but I want to see how it is [today]," he said.

Said Red Sox manager Jimy Williams: "He got hit in the back of the leg, but I thought he was moving around pretty good afterwards. He'll probably be OK."

Garciaparra stayed in the game last night—a good thing, considering his hit-robbing leap to grab a Jorge Posada line drive in the ninth inning.

But covered over, however slightly, by last night's medical alert was Garciaparra's 2-for-4, two-double, one-RBI performance. The second double—a shot down the left-field line—temporarily raised Garciaparra's average to an even .400.

"The kid can hit—I said that four years ago," said a beaming Williams. "This is one fine player. You people here get the chance to see him play a lot, and it has to be satisfying."

"I've seen three home runs before, but never 10 RBIs. And two grand slams. That's impressive. I think he's got a future," said Mark Portugal.

Lack of Chemistry the Missing Link for Nomar

By Tony Massarotti

Nomar Garciaparra chose his words with precision, measuring each question carefully as he went through his standard pregame routine. Garciaparra is completing his fourth full season with the Red Sox now. He has been nothing if not cautious, deliberate, downright systematic.

So when Garciaparra offers his insights and analyses on the disappointing 2000 Red Sox, it is imperative to read between the lines.

"What went wrong?" Garciaparra said, posing a rhetorical question last night at Comiskey Park, where the Red Sox began their final road trip of the season with a meaningless game against the Chicago White Sox.

"I think there's just a lot of stuff that happened over the course of the year—stuff that you hope doesn't happen—and it affected the team. Injuries happen a lot of times, but we can overcome injuries. A lot of faces came in and out the door, and when there's no stability—and I'm not saying it's the manager—but losing some key players, guys that aren't here anymore and are no longer with us, that has an effect.

"It takes a lot more than just putting talent out there on the field," Garciaparra said. "I think that's a big thing for our team—the chemistry and the camaraderie—that was there last year. That was a big thing for our team."

So there is another name on general manager Dan Duquette's rapidly expanding list of critics, it seems, though it is important to stress that Garciaparra last night never mentioned the GM by name. He never said anything overtly critical or inflammatory, either, because, generally speaking, that is not Garciaparra's way.

But listen to Garciaparra talk for just five minutes about the Red Sox and you *just know* that he has left Fenway Park shaking his head most nights, especially of late. You *just know* that he is disgusted by the actions of center fielder Carl Everett, even if it was Darren Lewis who confronted Everett in the Red Sox clubhouse last week. And you *just know* that his current support lies almost exclusively with his manager, Williams, under whom Garciaparra has played all but 24 games of his 592 career regular season games.

That said, let's clear up a couple of things. When Garciaparra speaks of "key players, guys that aren't here anymore," he is talking about Mike Stanley. Released by the Sox at midseason, Stanley may very well be going to the postseason as member of the Oakland A's. More than a few teammates (including Garciaparra) spoke on Stanley's behalf when the player was cut loose, and one member of the Sox coaching staff recently expressed his belief that Stanley's departure "[screwed] us up but good."

The instability? A clear reference to Duquette, particularly when Garciaparra went out of his way to absolve Williams.

After all, isn't it tough to manage with a revolving door to the club-house, too?

"Without a doubt," Garciaparra said. "It's hard to manage. What do I have to work with? Who do I have here today? That's difficult.

"I don't know all the stuff that's going on, but I've enjoyed playing under him," Garciaparra said of his manager. "I support him 100 percent. I have the utmost respect for him."

As for the flaps surrounding Everett, make of this what you may:

"As a player you may not always agree [with the manager], but you respect and do what he says because he *is* the manager," Garciaparra said. "I understand this game fully. You do it more on feel sometimes than you do by stats or numbers. You can have a righty hit for a righty, and if it doesn't work everybody says, 'Why didn't you pinch hit [a lefty]?' Well, maybe [the manager] just felt something, so you've got to respect that."

Understand?

During his time in Boston, Garciaparra has often been described by team-mates as someone who leads by example. Though he has expressed his share of frustration, he generally bit his tongue on most issues. There are some, undoubtedly, who would like him to be more vocal on issues, though that doesn't mean he lacks opinions.

It just means he doesn't express them at every turn, which is probably why he dodged the question when asked to comment on the team's personnel decisions this year.

"I don't make those decisions. I can't make those decisions, because, at the same time, I'm focused on what I do," Garciaparra said. "I can't say that because that's their job. I can't say, 'This is the way it should be.'"

Then again, maybe he doesn't have to.

Numbers Speak Volumes

By Jeff Horrigan

After collecting two hits in Friday's deflating elimination loss to the Tampa Bay Devil Rays, a crestfallen Nomar Garciaparra told Jimy Williams that if he wanted to rest him, he was comfortable with the idea.

The Red Sox manager knew that his shortstop, who had a 17-point lead over Anaheim's Darin Erstad, had locked up his second consecutive American League batting title, but he realized that another significant goal was attainable. With 197 hits after Friday, Garciaparra needed three hits in the final two games to become the first Red Sox player since Wade Boggs in the 1980s (seven straight times, 1983-89) to record consecutive 200-hit seasons.

"I talked with Nomar about it, and this kid has given his heart and soul for us every day," Williams said. "If he wanted those numbers, he'd tell me."

Garciaparra remained on the bench for the Sox' 4-2 victory at Tropicana Field yesterday, but even without the 200 hits, his 2000 season will go down as one of the greatest hitting displays in recent history.

Later today, he officially will become the first right-handed batter to win consecutive American League batting titles since Joe DiMaggio in 1939 and '40. He will also lead the league in road batting average (.370), night game batting average (.368) and batting average vs. right-handed pitching (.369).

"This is some hitter we're watching," said Williams. "We're very lucky."

Luck isn't a word normally associated with Garciaparra, unless it's preceded by bad. His home run total over the past three years fell from 35 to 27 to 21, but anyone who regularly attended games at Fenway Park this season can attest that the Green Monster robbed him of no less than 10 homers that would have been out at any other park.

"Everything he hits is just a bullet," teammate Lou Merloni said. "He's unbelievable. He hits the ball hard more consistently than anybody."

"Fans in Boston are going to appreciate the defense, because fans in Boston appreciate good baseball."

Healing Nomar Returns to Fenway

By Michael Silverman

Ten days after surgery to his right wrist, Nomar Garciaparra's progress was determined to be satisfactory by team doctor Bill Morgan.

"Everything looked good, no problems," Morgan said last night after examining Garciaparra and replacing his cast. The swelling was as expected and there was no infection in the incision made to repair his ECU tendon and smooth a bone, a procedure that will keep Garciaparra out of action for what is expected to be the first half of the season.

"My condition right now is that I'm in a cast; it's not going to heal in a week," Garciaparra said after the Red Sox' 8-2 victory over Baltimore last night. "How long's it going to take? I don't know."

Garciaparra returned yesterday from visiting his family in Southern California. Whenever there has not been a rolling power blackout, he has been watching most of the Red Sox games.

"The team's playing well, but it's always hard not to be out there," Garciaparra said. "It's frustrating, period, when you can't play."

Can't Rush Greatness

By Karen Guregian

He's been lobbing tennis balls against the wall for about 10 minutes a day and air-swinging with a fungo bat with his surgically repaired right wrist. Next comes tossing lightly with a baseball, and maybe, making contact with the ball off a batter's tee.

A smiling Nomar Garciaparra called this progress yesterday. As for us, we call it torture. Naturally, we wanted more from the Sox shortstop. We expected to see him in his familiar No. 5 Red Sox uniform, taking grounders and lobbing whatever choice of ball to first base. We've been crossing off days on the calendar since his April 2 surgery, anxiously awaiting a sign that Nomar—and his wrist—were well on the road back.

Hints were actually dropped in St. Petersburg, Fla., from manager Jimy Williams, of all people, that we would have more than a Nomar sighting yesterday. All we got was five minutes of Nomar in workout clothes in the outfield, casually tossing to a trainer.

We were led to believe we'd have a nice visual of him playing catch with his teammates yesterday.

Instead, we got Nomar Unplugged.

Given the way important news is disseminated to the media by this team, this development was hardly surprising. Garciaparra indicated he had no intention of doing anything on the field with the team prior to the game yesterday. He's simply not at that stage yet. Go figure.

All the miscommunications aside, it was nice to actually listen to Garciaparra talk about where he's at and see how the wrist looked up close and personal.

It's still not very pretty to view, with the fresh scar extending over the wrist bone where the torn tendon was repaired. Garciaparra, however, can now do simple tasks without difficulty. Yesterday, he opened mail, shook hands with the proper hand, and put on a pair of tight-fitting sports socks, muscling them up over his calves, using the wrist with no problem.

When asked if he was able to drive a standard, Nomar cracked: "I couldn't do that when I was healthy."

As for his baseball-like tasks, Garciaparra is slowly, but surely, making strides. He endures pain, even with light tossing, but maintains it's all part of the process.

"It's been feeling OK," said Garciaparra, who no longer wears a brace. "I still have some soreness. I still get pain. Throwing has been pretty difficult for me. It's been very tough. There's definitely a lot of pain doing that, but that's to be expected. It's nothing shocking. It's nothing new. The good thing is, it's progressively going down every time I do it.

"It's been recovering great," he said. "There hasn't been any swelling or setbacks. So everything I've been doing has been going forward in the right way."

He suggested he might be to the point of taking part in some in-field drills in a few days, but only in the way of fielding grounders. He's also itching to swing a real weighted bat, and yesterday, he reportedly did some work in the batting cage behind center field.

"At batting practice I might take ground balls. My legs are fine. I can do that," said Nomar, "but I'm not even close to throwing the ball, or throwing across the field. I'm barely lobbing the ball. I'm just working it out from there."

While dates of a possible return have been tossed around, specifically after the All-Star break July 9, Garciaparra calmly shot each and every date down. In his mind, there is no timetable. Just baby steps toward his ultimate goal of returning as a full-time player.

"Right now, everything is progressing the way it's supposed to," Garciaparra kept saying. "Everything is coming along great. I'm feeling good. I'm in great shape. I've been happy with my progression. It's taking baby steps. I'm not taking giant steps. It's baby steps, and as long as the baby steps are going forward and not backward, we're all right."

The team is in first place and has somehow functioned without him. That's why it's so tantalizing to imagine what it'd be like with him in there in the not-so-distant near future.

"I think everyone knows me. They know I'll be out there as soon as I can," he said. "My wrist will tell me more than anything when it's capable of handling the game."

In other words, don't believe anything you hear, especially if it comes from someone's mouth other than his.

Hot Nomar Heads Home

By Tony Massarotti

Precisely five months ago to the day, on Feb. 28, he stood in front of his locker at the Red Sox' minor-league training facility in Fort Myers, Fla., and spoke of the pain that had returned to his right wrist. He said he was "concerned," an uncharacteristic admission that stripped away spirit and triggered a wave of worry.

Today, anxiety has given way to anticipation.

Today, Nomar Garciaparra is quite literally making his way toward Boston.

And he looks ready to go.

"Yeah, I'm excited. I want to come back," Garciaparra said last night at Victory Field, where he went 3 for 5 with a single, double and home run in his fourth and final game of a rehabilitation assignment with the Triple A Pawtucket Red Sox.

"The team's doing well. It would be nice to come back and play. I want to be able to go out and help 'em and play my game. That's the important thing."

Excited? You bet. After going 2 for 3 with a crisp single and a supersonic double on Thursday night, Garciaparra arrived for last night's game and again found his name atop the lineup card. He reported "some swelling" in his right wrist, but nothing out of the ordinary, "nothing that affects me," and "stuff that is going to be there." He said he would decide during the game if he would play seven innings or nine, offering assurance that the decision had nothing to do with the health of his right wrist.

As it was, he came out of the game in the middle of the seventh, after flying to center in his final at-bat in the top of the inning.

Of course, had there been any doubt, Garciaparra would not have been in the lineup at all. And he probably would not have been on the field for batting practice, fielding ground balls and playfully flipping throws behind his back, bouncing around the diamond as if he had been allowed on the lawn for the very first time.

Certainly, he would not have opened the game by pounding a pitch from former teammate and current Indianapolis starter Tim Harikkala over the head of center fielder Lou Collier for his second clothesline double in as many nights. In his next two at-bats, Garciaparra homered to left and singled to center. In the field, he made one play in the hole, one charging toward the mound and one up the middle, where he did a pirouette before throwing a laser to first.

All three throws, in fact, were blow darts.

"I felt like I could have finished [the game], but it wasn't necessary . . . At this point, I don't think I have to play nine [innings] to tell me something," said Garciaparra, who went 7 for 16 in the series with all seven hits coming in his last 11 at-bats. "Being able to go out there and get back into it, I've been encouraged. There are going to be days where it's tired and it can't withstand the load, but the fact it's been able to withstand the load (so far) has been great.

"Your goal is to get back there and play. I think we've been very smart [in his rehabilitation]. I think I've been ahead of schedule in my mind with what we expected to do, but we've still got to be smart. For the most part, [his wrist] has been able to handle everything we've thrown at it."

As things stand, slightly more than 16 weeks have passed since Garciaparra underwent surgery on his right wrist on April 2, the date of the Red Sox' Opening Day loss to the Baltimore Orioles. During spring training, Red Sox general manager Dan Duquette placed Garciaparra's return to the club at

"10 to 16 weeks" from surgery, an estimate that aligned Garciaparra for a return on or near Aug. 1. That date arrives Wednesday.

As for Garciaparra, he will almost certainly be back on the field at Fenway Park sooner. He is not sure whether team doctor Bill Morgan will examine him today or tomorrow, as originally planned. But while Garciaparra continued to suggest that he would probably not play this weekend, the Red Sox have said nothing definitive about keeping Garciaparra out of the lineup tomorrow, a decision which might make sense because it would allow Garciaparra a day of rest on Monday, an open date.

"I haven't really thought about it," Garciaparra said when asked about the reception he might receive upon stepping into the batter's box for the first time this season at Fenway Park. "I'll deal with that when it comes to it. I've just been thinking about coming back."

Lately, with respect to him, most everyone in Boston has been doing the same.

"I love playing.
Nothing gives me
greater joy than
being on the field
and playing against
the best. Every kid
grows up wanting to
play against the
best."

Garciaparra's Back—and So Is His Bat

By Tony Massarotti

Just before his final at-bat, he rose from his seat and lowered his head, walking the length of the dugout as he made the sign of the cross. Nomar Garciaparra put on a helmet and grabbed a bat, then walked up the dugout steps to answer all those prayers.

Nomar's back.

And he's already swinging a big stick.

Hallelujah.

"He's a one-of-a-kind player," Red Sox warhorse David Cone said after Garciaparra hit a two-out, two-run single in the bottom of the seventh inning to propel the Red Sox to a 4-3 victory over the Chicago White Sox at Fenway Park yesterday in the team's latest fairy tale installment.

"You just don't do those sorts of things without being a different breed," Cone said. "There's a really short list of comparatives in terms of ballplayers. What he did [yesterday] was nothing short of remarkable. Words can't describe what he did after that kind of layoff and that kind of injury."

Said Sox manager Jimy Williams: "He has a very simple hitting approach; it's pretty simple what he does. It may be impossible to duplicate for other players, but it's very simple. He stays still, his eyes are still and then he has those [wrists]."

The Red Sox have missed a lot of things about Garciaparra this season. They have missed his full-spectrum fielding range and his high-octane throwing arm, his instincts on the bases and his mere, simple presence. Mostly they have missed his bat, which yesterday produced a 2 for 4 effort that included a home run, a game-winning single and three RBIs, despite the fact that Garciaparra had not faced a big-league pitcher in exactly 10 months.

Garciaparra played in just four minor-league games while on a rehabilitation assignment with Triple A Pawtucket last week. *Four*. He jumped from a virtual standstill into a playoff race, a task that one American League scout regarded as so difficult that he suggested the Red Sox were rushing Garciaparra back.

"I read where one guy said we were rushing him too much," Sox third base coach Gene Lamont said with a wide grin. "Tell him we did . . . by two at-bats."

Indeed, Garciaparra was hitless in his first two at-bats of the season when he stepped in against White Sox starter Sean Lowe in the bottom of the sixth with the White Sox holding a 2-1 lead. Garciaparra fouled off a first-pitch strike before Lowe fell behind 2- 1, a count that compelled the pitcher to throw a fastball over the heart of the plate.

Releasing his hands as if he had been coiled, Garciaparra belted the pitch into the center-field bleachers to tie the game. An

inning later, after both Chris Stynes and Trot Nixon failed with the bases loaded and Chicago holding a 3-2 lead, Garciaparra punched a single to center against reliever Gary Glover that turned a loss into a victory and turned Fenway on its ear.

For the Red Sox, the hit snapped a stretch during which the team went 0 for 14 with runners in scoring position. For Garciaparra, the hit improved his career average with the bases loaded to .413 with 66 RBIs in 63 at-bats. Since the start of the 1999 season, the wonderboy shortstop of the Red Sox is now batting .364 with runners in scoring position, .377 with runners in scoring position and two outs.

See what you've been missing?

"The key is he's such a great first-pitch hitter," Cone said when asked what made Garciaparra such an efficient hitter in the clutch. "When he steps into the box, he's ready to hit. Paul Molitor was like that and that really scares the pitcher out of the strike zone. You almost have to try to take an 0-2 approach on the first pitch [against him]. If you give him anything good at all to hit, he's going to pound it."

The cheers grew the loudest then, though they were only the last in a long sequence. Garciaparra was cheered when he stepped out of the dugout before the game, cheered when the starting lineups were announced, cheered when he went out to shortstop in the top of the first. He was cheered when he stepped into the batter's box for the first time, his first home game since Sept. 24.

And he was cheered in the seventh inning, with the game on the line, as he strode toward the batter's box with a bat in his hands.

"I kind of thought back to years past. Those are our fans. They're awesome," Garciaparra said. "I felt like, this is what I missed."

There were 33,375 fans at Fenway Park thinking exactly the same thing.

Comeback an Instant Classic

By Steve Buckley

You know how on special occasions, some teams use throwback uniforms? The Red Sox use throwback players. Each new day offers a little bit of yesterday, as another player, not seen for a long time, pulls on a uniform and reports for duty.

Friday night it was Bret Saberhagen, winning his first game since 1999. Saturday afternoon it was Carl Everett, late of the Gulf Coast League and the medic's table, back in the lineup for the first time since June 21.

Yesterday, it was the return of the team's poster boy, Nomar Garciaparra. When he trotted out to shortstop for the first time this season, his right wrist all better, his road trip to Indianapolis behind him, it was a singular Fenway moment, one for the scrapbooks and the video library.

No, it wasn't Tony Conigliaro in '69, or Henry Aaron making his American League debut, or even Bryce Florie strutting out to the mound in those funky black glasses. But understand this about Nomar Garciaparra: He belongs as much to the *game* as he belongs to the Red Sox, and the game will soon lose Tony Gwynn and Cal Ripken Jr.

In other words, the *game* can't afford to be without the few men who not only play it greatly, but passionately.

"He means a lot to the game, No. 1, or maybe it's the Red Sox No. 1 and the game No. 2," said Red Sox manager Jimy Williams, apparently still debating the issue with himself. "Play it any way you want.

"He plays the game right. He plays with *respect* to the game."

Garciaparra could have gone 0 for 4, and the Red Sox could have lost, and lost bad, and still, years from now, those fans who were in attendance yesterday would have been saying, "That first game Nomar played back in '01 . . . now THAT was really something."

But Nomar did not go 0 for 4. He crushed a home run that landed in the front row of the center-field bleachers, and then in the seventh inning with the Red Sox down

by a run, he lined a two-run single up the middle. And the Red Sox won, topping the White Sox 4-3.

There are times when players get too guarded about these moments and refuse to 'fess up and admit that, yeah, it is *special*. But this was not one of those times, because Nomar, in his postgame chat with the media, talked about as fast as Tommy Harper, circa 1965, going from first to third on a single to right. In other words, yes, yes, yes, Nomar knew it was special . . . and was delighted to tell you so.

"I love playing the game," he said. "The game puts a smile on my face. I enjoy being out there."

Had he slept the night before? Or perhaps he was wandering the streets all night, maybe sitting on a beach somewhere, pondering his future, wondering if the surgically repaired wrist is ready for the big-league grind.

"I was able to sleep," he said. "And that surprised me, that I was able to sleep. But as I was driving to the park, it began to hit me . . . all the nervousness, anxiety. Sort of like playing in my first big-league game. I was thinking, it's really going to happen."

His teammates surely knew what was going on inside Garciaparra's head. But David Cone, Boston's starting pitcher, had to know *more*. This is a guy who, in 1996, after suffering an aneurysm in his right arm, returned to the mound and threw seven no-hit innings against the Oakland A's.

"He played, what, four rehab games and he comes out and does that?" asked Cone. "That's a natural. He's a one-of-a-kind player. It's just that short of remarkable. I can't remember seeing anything quite as dramatic as what I saw today. You almost become a fan in the dugout."

Nomar Garciaparra is not a quote machine. He is not clever with the one-liners, doesn't tell funny stories. Like Ted Williams and Carl Yastrzemski and Jim Rice before him, he feels no need to hold daily court with the writers.

But he does feel a need to play the game with a vengeance, and, well, a question: How many big-leaguers these days truly play the game with a vengeance?

Gwynn and Ripken are stepping out, and it's time for the Nomar Garciaparras of the world to step up. For the Red Sox, sure, but also for the game.

MRI for Nomar

By Jeff Horrigan

The Red Sox insist that there is no reason to panic, but Nomar Garciaparra was back in Boston last night due to recurring wrist problems while the team opened the most vital 13-game stretch of the season at Jacobs Field.

Garciaparra flew home late Monday afternoon and was examined yesterday by team physician Dr. Bill Morgan, who arranged for a magnetic resonance imaging test on his surgically repaired right wrist.

The two-time defending American League batting champion didn't play in Saturday's 18-inning loss in Texas, but the prearranged night off from manager Joe Kerrigan did nothing to dispel the pain and discomfort that lingered after Friday's game. Garciaparra nevertheless played on Sunday and went 0 for 4 with a strikeout and an error in a 5-4 loss to the Texas Rangers.

Kerrigan spoke with Garciaparra on the flight from Dallas to Cleveland on Sunday night, and it was decided that he would return to Boston for further tests.

"We need to get peace of mind, not only for him but for us," Kerrigan said.

Garciaparra, who had surgery to repair a damaged ligament on April 2, evidently was experiencing great discomfort over the weekend but didn't disclose it until after Sunday's game.

"Coming off 18 innings, he felt an obligation to play, a duty to play," Kerrigan said. "Because of the type of man he is, he kept [the pain] to himself."

Mike Lansing said it was no secret in the clubhouse that Garciaparra was hurting.

"He wants to play and help this team," Lansing said. "Everyone plays in pain, but he's endured a lot, and it probably got to be a little too much."

Garciaparra, who was activated from the disabled list on July 29, has hit .289 with four home runs and eight RBIs in 21 games. It was clear over the weekend, however, that the wrist was still bothering him.

"Everything he hits is just a bullet," said Lou Merloni. "He's unbelievable. He hits the ball hard more consistently than anybody."

Nomar Muscles into Camp

By Jeff Horrigan

Nomar Garciaparra reported for duty yesterday insisting that his Adonis-like body is more buff than ever before.

After being limited to 21 games last season following the difficult recovery from surgery to repair a damaged tendon in his right wrist, the Red Sox shortstop released his pent-up aggression in an off-season workout regimen that began in October and ended over the weekend.

Even though he claims to be bigger and stronger than ever before, the general public is going to have to take his word for it. The two-time American League batting champion won't be showing off his chiseled frame anytime soon.

One day after appearing bare-chested on the cover of *Sports Illustrated* last spring, Garciaparra discovered that he had suffered a longitudinal split of his ECU tendon. The fabled *SI* cover jinx has led the superstitious 28-year-old to become more self-conscious of his bare physique than El Guapo in a Speedo.

"You guys [in the media] are going to notice it when you see me take my shirt off," he said of his added muscle, "but that's it . . . no pictures this year."

Garciaparra became the first right-handed hitter to win consecutive AL batting titles since Joe DiMaggio in 1939-40 when he paced the league with a career-high .372 average in 2000. Shortly after arriving for spring training last year, however, it became clear he wasn't going to have the opportunity to three-peat.

Garciaparra said the wrist didn't bother him during his workouts in Phoenix but anticipated the return of some minor swelling and discomfort due to the fact that he is only 10 1/2 months removed from surgery.

"I'm sure it will come as we do more and intensify things, but I don't expect it to bother me much," he said. "It's been feeling pretty good, but I've got to be smart."

Nomar Thins Out

By *Boston Herald* Staff

Before the wrist injury, there were muscle pulls, ligament strains, an assortment of nagging problems that too often kept him off the field. Nomar Garciaparra now sounds and looks healthy, and he appears less like a runaway weightlifter and more like a wonderboy shortstop.

"He doesn't look huge," observed former Red Sox manager and current Houston Astros skipper Jimy Williams.

That wasn't so true a year ago. Coming off a second consecutive American League batting title, Garciaparra arrived at spring training last season looking like The Rock. Garciaparra always has been sensitive about his physique and workout regimen. In his mind, the home runs and muscles were a package deal, and nobody ever claimed he was too bulked up when he was trotting around the bases.

Yet there were those who wondered whether Garciaparra's rash of ailments was the result of extra-large muscles on a medium frame. Garciaparra's wrist injury was initially caused by being hit by a pitch, but many of his other problems have been sprains and strains, suggesting his body may have been overtaxed.

Whatever the reasons, Garciaparra arrived in camp this year roughly "five pounds" lighter than a year ago, though opposing scouts believe he looks even leaner. He is not nearly as thick through his shoulders and chest and insisted he has merely "redistributed" weight throughout his frame.

Though he is somewhat cryptic about the precise reasons for the physical changes, Garciaparra acknowledged that he modified a typically intense off-season conditioning program to help minimize the chance of injury.

"Absolutely. I never want to be off the field. [Staying healthy] is what you try to do, but I won't change the way I play, too," Garciaparra said. "You work to keep the strength, the flexibility and the power. And you want to do stuff for injury prevention."

If spring training was any indication, the results have been encouraging.

Shortstop's Health Helps Sox Wealth

By Tony Massarotti

For all of the numbers he is amassing, the most important one for Nomar Garciaparra this season remains indisputable. The wonderboy shortstop of the Red Sox has played in 50 of his team's 53 games to date, more than anyone else on the club except third baseman Shea Hillenbrand.

And if that trend continues, rest assured that the other numbers will come along, too.

"You look at the guys who are big and strong and have all those power numbers, but do they get hurt?" Garciaparra said. "I think I would rather be out there [on the field]."

Early summer has been an interesting time for baseball, with the disclosure of steroid use in the major leagues. This prompted a wave of discussion throughout the game, including the never-ending debate about the relevance of strength in the batter's box.

Garciaparra's physique has always been a touchy issue for the player, who has missed an average of better than 52 games a season since playing 153 in his rookie year. Much of that can be attributed to wrist surgery that forced Garciaparra to miss 141 games last year, but the truth is that he also had grown more susceptible to nagging injuries as he packed on bulk as if it were bubble wrap.

A muscled-up coverboy for *Sports Illustrated* in the spring of 2001, Garciaparra modified his training regimen last winter and showed up in camp with noticeably less bulk on his frame. He acknowledged then that part of his strategy was to limit the injuries that have kept an otherwise healthy and well-conditioned 28-year- old off the field for far too many games, which means Garciaparra started to use a different muscle that too many players have ignored.

His brain.

"I think [injuries] were kind of both of our concerns going into the off season. It gets to a point where you only have to be so strong to play this game," said Red Sox

infielder Lou Merloni, who works out with Garciaparra during the winter. "The focus was more on flexibility and agility and staying healthy.

"In past years, we lifted and got to the point where we trying to add more power, and maybe that contributed to some nagging injuries. I don't know if he lost any strength [this year]. He just keeps going."

That has been especially true of late, a period during which Garciaparra has built his latest 10-game hitting streak, the incredible 18th such string of his career. During that span he is batting .425 with 17 hits, 11 RBIs, eight runs scored, five doubles, three home runs and a triple. And he has done it all without the benefit of Manny Ramirez batting behind him.

With one-third of the schedule complete, Garciaparra is on pace to post some of the best totals in his career. Though he has just eight home runs, his 32 extra-base hits rank second in the majors behind only Yankees second baseman Alfonso Soriano. Garciaparra's slugging percentage is .574, in line with his career number of .570, and he is on pace to finish with 202 hits, 122 runs scored, 134 RBIs, 64 doubles, nine triples and 24 home runs.

And, perhaps, most importantly, 153 games played.

"People have been asking about his batting average and his power, but the guy was hurt for a year. Ask a pitcher the year after he had elbow surgery and is he throwing as hard? No," said Merloni. "I think it's the same thing with Nomar. But he's a couple of months deep now and he really seems to be swinging it in the last two weeks."

As long as Garciaparra stayed in the lineup, there really never should have been a doubt.

Photo Credits

The following photographers from the staff of the *Boston Herald* Photography Department contributed to this book. We gratefully acknowledge the efforts of:

Bill Belknap
Renee DeKona
Mark Garfinkel
Jim Mahoney
George Martell
Ren Norton
Michael Seamans
Matt Stone
Laurie Swope
Kuni Takahashi
Matthew West
John Wilcox

Technical support: **Darlene Sarno**

Chief Photographer: **Jon Landers**
Assistant Director of Photography: **Ted Anchor**
Assistant Director of Photography: **Arthur Pollack**
Director of Photography: **Garo Lachinian**